Right Plant, Right Place

Jackie Matthews

HERMES
HOUSE

The edition published by Hermes House

© Anness Publishing Limited 2002 updated 2003..

Hermes House is an imprint of Anness Publishing Limited,
Hermes House, 88–89 Blackfriars Road, London SE1 8HA

Publisher: Joanna Lorenz
Production Controller: Joanna King

Publisher's Note:
The Reader should not regard the recommendations, ideas and techniques
expressed and described in this book as substitutes for the advice of a
qualified medical practitioner or other qualified professional.
Any use to which the recommendations, ideas and techniques
are put is at the reader's sole discretion and risk.

Printed in Hong Kong/China

3 5 7 9 10 8 6 4

CONTENTS

Introduction

EVERY PLANT HAS A PREFERENCE ABOUT ITS IDEAL GROWING
CONDITIONS, AND PUTTING A PLANT IN THE RIGHT LOCATION AND
SOIL WILL ENSURE THAT IT HAS THE BEST POSSIBLE START
AND CHANCE OF LONG-TERM HEALTH AND VIGOUR.

PERFECT PLANT ENVIRONMENTS

Many factors influence the environment in your garden and conditions can vary considerably in different parts of it. The climate, type of soil, shelter and the amount of sunlight it receives all play a role.

Fortunately, many plants can cope with a wide range of climatic variation and soil, and grow surprisingly well in conditions far removed from their natural habitat. These plants are understandably popular and deserve to be considered for inclusion in many

Above: This fuchsia and clematis look good together, and the clematis also benefits from having its roots in the shade.

schemes. But to get the very best results in the long-term, plants need to be carefully selected to suit the particular conditions that are to be found in your garden, as well as to suit the requirements of your design.

ALTERING THE ENVIRONMENT

While it is always better to work with nature, rather than against it, sometimes you may want to influence it to allow you to grow particular plants. Altering the environment within your garden allows you to create microclimates specifically for certain types of plants to enjoy.

Above: A single garden can contain dozens of environments, each of which can be exploited by growing suitable plants.

SOIL STRUCTURE

All soil consists of sand, silt, clay and humus (organic matter), and the proportions in which each is present will determine its structure – its consistency and water-retaining properties. The more large sand particles it contains, the more easily water will drain through it and the quicker it will warm up in spring, allowing earlier planting. Silt particles are smaller, so water is held for longer, but they retain little in the way of nutrients. Clay particles are the smallest of all. They hold on to nutrients and water very well, but in high percentages will produce a heavy, solid soil that is cold (slow to warm up in spring), and prone to damage if worked when too wet.

Chalky and limy soils, which overlie chalk or limestone, are shallow,

Above: Matching plants to the type of soil in your garden ensures that they will thrive and perform well.

free-draining and of moderate fertility. Loam is a perfect balance of all the elements. It is a crumbly soil, often dark in colour, which holds both moisture and nutrients well without becoming waterlogged. Unfortunately, this ideal soil is rare, and most gardens have a soil that favours one particle size over the others and so needs help in the form of added organic matter.

Above: A small pond sunk into a patio allows water-loving plants to be grown in an otherwise dry situation.

GARDENER'S TIP

To find out the texture of your soil, pick up a handful of damp soil and roll it between your finger and thumb. If it feels rough and granular, but the grains don't adhere to each other, the soil is sandy. If it forms a ball when your roll it between your thumb and forefinger, it is a sandy loam. If it is rather sticky and makes a firm shape, it is a clay loam. But if you can mould it into shapes, it is a clay soil.

Above: Roses grow in most types of soil, but most prefer slightly acid conditions if they are to produce abundant blooms.

SOIL pH

A soil's calcium level (its pH) determines whether it is acid or alkaline and can vary considerably within even local areas, depending on where topsoil may have been brought in from or the nature of the underlying rock. Within a garden levels can vary depending on where manure, fertilizer, lime or even builder's rubble has been applied in the past.

Individual plants prefer different pH levels and some have quite specific requirements. It is a good idea to test the soil in your garden or border before selecting plants. You can then be sure to make an appropriate choice.

Altering pH levels

It is possible to influence the pH level in soil, although this is usually only worthwhile for growing vegetables when increasing yields is desirable. With ornamental plants it is usually more satisfactory to choose plants to suit the soil.

Raising soil pH is relatively easy and can have beneficial effects on a long-term basis, but lowering it is difficult, costly and usually only a short-term measure. If you really want to grow lime-hating plants and your soil has a pH reading of 7 or over, then the best option is probably to grow them in containers with a compost (soil mix) to suit.

Above: Foxgloves and many other cottage-garden plants are not fussy about the type of soil they grow in.

Above: Many plants, including ferns, will thrive in the moist area surrounding a fountain.

MOISTURE

Plants vary in the amount of moisture they require, and the amount of moisture available to plants in your garden will depend on a number of factors.

Rainfall can vary considerably within quite small areas depending on local topographical conditions, and even the direction in which the garden faces can affect the water it receives, depending on the prevailing wind relative to the house. Even though plenty of rain falls, it may not be falling on the soil where it is needed, but on the house, where it runs off down the drains.

How long the moisture is held within the soil, and therefore how long it is available for use by plants, is affected by the amount of sun or shade the plot receives as well as the soil type. A light, sandy soil loses its moisture quickly, while a heavy, clay soil is slower to drain, making moisture available to the plants for a longer period of time. Warmth from the sun will not only cause the soil to dry out more quickly, but will encourage plants to grow and use up more water.

Additionally, having large established specimens already in situ can mean there is less water available for newly introduced plants. An older plant will have sent roots down to the lower levels within the soil, to take advantage of all the moisture it can, leaving little for a new plant that is still reliant on water much nearer the surface. A 5-year-old tree, for example, will take up in excess of 4 litres (1 gallon) of water every day. If the garden does not receive enough rainfall to support plants with this kind of requirement you may have to consider choosing plants that need a lower intake.

Above: Ebullient yellow mimulas contrast well with the restrained foliage of hostas. Both these plants like moist soil.

Introduction

SUN AND SHADE

Light is essential to plants. It provides the energy needed by the plant to manufacture food during daylight hours, a process known as photosynthesis. The length of daylight also influences the time of year when flowers and fruit are produced and leaves fall.

The amount of light individual plants require varies. Although the majority of garden plants are sun loving, there are nonetheless plenty of shade-loving plants that will also thrive in darker conditions. Many even prefer to grow in shade. Mediterranean plants and roses grow best in direct sunlight, but rhododendrons like some shade. Ivies and periwinkles like heavily shaded areas.

Above: A sun-drenched border blazes with a breathtaking display of fiery reds and yellows.

WIND AND POLLUTION

Exposure to strong winds can be a problem for some plants, especially young ones or those with fragile stems. It can damage growth and cause desiccation. Conversely a gentle wind aids the dispersal of pollen and seed, can cool plants down in hot weather, and prevents the build-up of a stagnant atmosphere round plants, which can incubate disease. Where strong wind is a regular problem, it needs to be moderated by the installation of a windbreak of some sort.

Busy urban thoroughfares can become laden with fumes and particles that can be detrimental to many plants, especially in front gardens. Finding attractive specimens that can withstand this daily onslaught will ensure that an urban garden never looks drab.

Above: Many plants enjoy shady conditions, but they tend to lack colourful flowers. Here, a garden ornament adds interest.

Above: Clever use of plant colour and shape can create stunning effects in any location within a garden.

PLANNING YOUR PLANTING

Whether you are planning an entire garden or just designing a border, you will naturally begin by visualizing the effect you want to create, and listing favourite plants that you cannot do without. Before you go any further, and without compromising your initial vision, it is essential to check all their growing requirements and be realistic about what you can grow.

Hard surfaces, including raised beds and paths, and vertical elements, in the form of climbing plants, shrubs and trees, need careful consideration. These create microclimates, extending the range of plants you can grow.

Most plants look far better when planted in largish groups. Propagation is one of the easiest and cheapest ways to increase your stock of plants. But you will need to plan when to do this in order to have plants ready for your garden at the correct time. Most propagation is done in the autumn by taking cuttings or collecting seeds.

HOW TO USE THIS BOOK

This book explains how to successfully match plants to the conditions in your garden, in order to maximize good results. The first section tackles the basics of ground preparation, sowing and planting as well as offering tips on plant maintenance. In *Different Soil Conditions*, you can learn about how your soil influences the types of plants you are likely to grow most successfully. In *Planting in Different Locations* are examples of different types of site likely to exist within a garden and suggestions for planting them. Finally, there is a chart of plants with information on preferred soil type, position, planting and flowering time, and a list of common and Latin plant names.

Above: Planting in groups gives solid patches of eye-catching colour.

Getting Started

WHATEVER PLANTS YOU CHOOSE, YOU NEED TO LOOK AFTER THEM CORRECTLY. CAREFUL SOIL PREPARATION, SOWING AND PLANTING WILL PAY DIVIDENDS. REGULAR CHECKING AND MAINTENANCE ONCE ESTABLISHED WILL ENSURE THRIVING SPECIMENS.

ANALYSING YOUR SOIL

Plant nutrients are held in solution in the soil where they are absorbed by the roots. Phosphorus, potassium, magnesium, calcium and sulphur are needed in fairly large quantities for plants to thrive. Trace elements including manganese and chlorine are also needed in smaller quantities. You can test the soil for major nutrients using a special soil testing kit to see if any are lacking.

The calcium content of soil is measured on a scale of pH, which ranges from 0 to 14. The most acid is 0 and 14 is the most alkaline. The scale of pH affects the solubility of minerals and therefore their availability to plants via the roots.

Testing for pH

Before selecting plants for your garden, it is worth testing your soil to see whether it is acid, neutral or alkaline. A pH soil testing kit is easy to use and readily available from a garden centre. Alternatively, you can use a pH meter, which has a probe for inserting into the soil and is more economical in the long term.

1 Take a sample of soil from the area to be tested from about 10 cm (4 in) under the soil surface. If it is wet, allow it to dry out. Place the sample in a screw-top jar or test tube.

2 Following the manufacturer's instructions, add the indicator chemical to the soil and then the liquid. Shake vigorously and allow the contents to settle. Repeat the shaking and allow to settle again. Compare the colour of the liquid to the chart accompanying the kit to find the pH level of your soil. It is best to test several samples from different parts of the garden, as pH can vary within quite a small area. It can also alter over time, so repeat the process every few years to give you an accurate reading of current conditions.

Preparing the Soil

The best results are achieved by getting the growing site in as good a condition as possible before you even purchase or propagate a plant. Once plants are in the soil, it will be difficult to dig it over or add compost in bulk. The first task is to clear the ground. The most likely problem will be weeds, but in many new gardens there will be builder's rubbish to remove.

Weeds have to be either totally removed or killed. If the soil in your garden is light and crumbly, it is possible to remove the weeds as you dig. On heavier soils you can either cover the ground with an impermeable mulch such as thick black polythene, for several months, or use a weedkiller.

Dig the soil over, adding as much well-rotted organic matter as possible. If you can, carry out the digging in the autumn and leave the ground until spring before planting. If you do this you will see, and be able to remove, any weeds that have re-grown from roots that were missed before.

For an existing bed top-dress the soil with a good layer of well-rotted compost or farmyard manure.

GARDENER'S TIP

Never attempt to work soil when the weather is very wet. Pressure on wet soil will compact it. If you do have to get on a border when it is wet, stand on a wooden plank, which spreads the load.

Digging a New Bed

1 When the ground is cleared of weeds, dig the first trench to one spade's depth across the plot. Barrow the soil to the other end of the plot.

2 Fork a layer of well-rotted compost or manure into the bottom of the trench to improve the soil structure and provide nutrients for the plants. Break it up if it is in thick clumps.

3 Dig the next trench across the plot, turning the soil on to the compost in the first trench. Add compost to the new trench and then dig the next. Continue down the border until the whole surface has been turned. Fill the final trench with the earth taken from the first.

SOWING SEED IN SOIL

For bulk growing of the more common garden plants, sowing directly into the soil is far less bother and much less expensive because you will not need to buy pots and compost (soil mix).

Like annuals, many perennials can be sown where they are to flower, but for those that will not flower until the following year it is best to sow them in a nursery bed, if you have the space.

Sow the seed in spring, as the soil begins to warm up. You can bring this forward a few weeks if you cover the soil with cloches from early spring. Mark the ends of each row with labels so you know what you have planted. Do not let the bed dry out and keep it weeded. When the seedlings have grown to a manageable size, thin them to distances of at least 15cm (6in).

Most species will be ready to plant out in their flowering position during the following autumn while the ground is still warm.

EASY SEED FOR SOWING IN OPEN GROUND

Alcea
Aquilegia
Astrantia
Centranthus ruber
Delphinium
Foeniculum
Helleborus
Myosotis
Primula
Verbascum
Verbena
Viola

SOWING IN OPEN GROUND

1 Prepare the soil carefully, removing all weeds and breaking it down into a fine tilth with a rake.

2 Draw out a shallow drill with a corner of a hoe, about 1cm ($\frac{1}{2}$in) deep. Keep the drill straight by using a garden line as a guide. If the soil is dry, water the drill with a watering can and wait until the water has soaked in.

3 Sow the seed thinly along the drill. Larger seed can be sown at intervals to avoid the need for thinning later. Gently rake the soil back into the drill, covering over the seed. Tamp down the row with the base of the rake. Keep the drills moist until germination.

SOWING SEED IN POTS

For small quantities of seeds, and those that can be difficult to germinate, such as parsley, sow in 9cm (3¹/₂in) pots or in a tray, then place in a sheltered spot, away from direct sun. Germination will usually take from a few days to a few weeks depending on the species, although some can take longer and may even require a winter's cold weather before germination will occur. Keep the pots watered. The seedlings are ready to prick out when they have developed their first true leaves or when they are large enough to handle. Keep them covered in a cold frame for a day or so, before hardening them off by gradually opening the frame more fully each day.

Most perennials can be sown in early spring. Some, however, such as primulas and hellebores, need to be sown as soon as the seeds ripen in late summer or autumn.

SOWING SEED IN CONTAINERS

1 Fill a pot or tray with compost (soil mix). Tap firmly on the bench to settle the compost and lightly flatten the surface with the base of a pot. This will exclude air pockets which would hinder the growth of roots. Sow the seed thinly on top.

2 Cover the seed with a layer of sieved compost or fine gravel. Water the pot thoroughly either from above with a watering can fitted with a fine rose or from below by standing the pot in a tray of shallow water.

PRICKING OUT SEEDLINGS

1 Water the pot an hour before gently knocking out the seedlings. Carefully break up the rootball and split into clumps. Dealing with one clump at a time, gently ease the seedlings away, touching only the leaves.

2 Hold a seedling over a pot by one or more of its leaves and gently trickle moist compost around its roots until the pot is full. Avoid touching the fragile stem or roots. Tap the pot on the bench to exclude any air pockets, then firm down gently with your fingertips and water.

Getting Started

Buying Plants

Most plants are available in containers all year round. If you want good-quality plants that are accurately labelled, go to a reputable source.

Check your prospective purchase carefully and reject any plant that is diseased, looks unhealthy or is harbouring pests. If possible, knock it out of its pot and look at the roots. Again reject any that show signs of pests. Also reject any that are pot-bound, that is when the roots have wound round the inside of the pot, creating a solid mass. Such plants are difficult to establish.

If the plants are in a greenhouse or tunnel, harden them off when you get them home. Planting them straight out in the garden may put them under stress, from which they might not recover.

Above: Bulbs are invaluable for growing in borders as well as for naturalizing in grassy areas.

Planting Bulbs

Much of the interest and colour in a spring garden comes from flowering bulbs. Daffodils, tulips, snowdrops, bluebells, crocuses, *Iris reticulata*, aconites and hyacinths can be used en masse in borders or singly under trees. Daffodils, crocuses, bluebells and aconites can be naturalized in lawns. To plant in lawns remove a plug of grass and soil and replace after positioning the bulbs.

Planting Bulbs in a Border

1 Excavate a hole large enough to take a group of bulbs. If the soil is poor or impoverished fork in garden compost or well-rotted manure. You could also add a layer of grit or sand.

2 Space out the bulbs, not too evenly, planting at a depth that will leave them covered with about twice their own depth of soil.

3 To deter slugs and encourage the bulbs to flower sprinkle more grit or sand around them before returning the soil.

Planting Shrubs and Perennials

When you are planting a new border put all the plants, still in their pots, in their positions according to your planting plan. Stand back to assess the result and make any necessary adjustments. When you are satisfied with the positions of the plants you can begin to plant.

Water the plants before planting out. Start planting at the back or one end of a border and move forwards. When you have finished planting, cover the soil between the plants with a layer of mulch to keep the weeds down and preserve moisture. Be prepared to water regularly in dry weather for at least the first few weeks after planting. If you are planting isolated plants in unprepared soil, add plenty of well-rotted organic matter to the soil.

If you decide that a plant is in the wrong spot you may have to leave it in place for the growing season, otherwise you might damage the roots, but in autumn or spring, you can lift it and mover it to a better position.

SPRING BULBS

Crocus
Cyclamen coum
Eranthis hyemalis
Galanthus nivalis
Hyacinthoides
Hyacinthus
Iris reticulata
Narcissus
Tulipa

Planting Out

1 Dig a hole with a trowel or spade, and with the plant still in its pot, check that the depth and width is right. The plant must be placed in the soil at the same depth that it was in the pot or just a little deeper.

2 Knock the plant out of its pot, tease out some of the roots, to help them become established in the ground more quickly, and place it in the planting hole. Fill around the plant with soil and then firm it with your hands or a heel to expel large pockets of air. Water thoroughly unless the weather is wet. Mulch the surface with chipped bark, gravel, leaf mould or compost.

Maintaining Your Plants

Deadheading, pruning, mulching, feeding and watering all need to be done from time to time to keep your plants in good order.

Mulching

To keep annual weeds down and conserve moisture and warmth, it is useful to cover the soil surface with a mulch, such as garden compost, well-rotted manure or composted bark chippings. As worms distribute the organic matter, soil structure and fertility will also be improved. Do not apply mulch in cold weather, as it will insulate the cold conditions, but wait until the soil has warmed up in spring.

Remove perennial weeds and water the ground thoroughly before applying the mulch. Do not apply a mulch to dry ground. Spread the mulch thickly, about 5cm (2in) deep, to prevent light reaching weed seeds.

Above: Always use well-rotted organic matter, otherwise it will extract nitrogen from the soil in the process of breaking down.

Above: Use a watering can with a fine rose for smaller areas. A large border will need a garden hose.

Watering

Newly planted shrubs and perennials need to be watered well during the first growing season. Water as much as you can during very dry seasons, but try to do this in the early morning or late in the day, when the plants are not in full sun. Otherwise their leaves may get scorched. On really hot days, this might mean waiting until well after sunset to give the garden any real benefit from watering.

Make sure the ground is thoroughly soaked. If you only wet the surface the plants will tend to form shallow roots, rather than seeking water from deep in the soil.

Feeding

If you thoroughly prepare the ground before planting and then top-dress with organic matter, sufficient nutrients

Above: Roses in particular appreciate regular deadheading to keep them looking tidy and encourage more blooms.

should be available to the plants, and there should be no need for further feeding until the following year. If you do not have access to much organic matter, such as farmyard manure or spent mushroom compost, apply a light feed of a general balanced fertilizer in spring. If the plants look particularly starved, try a liquid feed.

Deadheading

As soon as the blooms of annuals and perennials have died, remove them to encourage new ones to form and prolong the flowering season. Regular deadheading also keeps plants looking tidy by removing unsightly dying vegetation. However, if the flowers go on to produce attractive seedpods that will extend the ornamental attributes of the plant, leave them to mature.

Some perennials, such as delphiniums and phlox, can be cut back after the first flush of flowers to encourage the growth of side shoots. A second flowering will appear on these later developing shoots.

Pruning

Many shrubs are pruned annually to improve the supply of new shoots that will produce flowers more readily than old wood. Pruning also keeps shrubs compact and in good shape. The correct time to prune depends on the type of flowering wood. Plants that flower in spring and early summer usually do so on the previous year's growth, so they need to be pruned after flowering. Those that flower after midsummer usually do so on the current year's growth and are pruned in early spring.

The precise pruning requirements vary according to the species, so consult a guide before you begin.

Above: Cut out crossing stems while they are still young. Cut the stem at its base where it joins the main branch.

Different Soil Conditions

Soils vary widely in their level of acidity or alkalinity and the structure of their particles, which range from light sand to heavy clay. These factors determine how much moisture and nutrients they contain.

Acid Soil

This type of soil can be free draining and sandy, heavy and sticky, or even organic with a high peat content. Clay soils are often acid, and peaty soils, where the organic matter has not decomposed, are almost always acid.

Some soils, even if originally alkaline, can gradually become more acid as a result of the lime being washed out of the upper layers close to the soil

Above: Spectacular camellias prefer acid soil, where they can grow to the size of a small tree.

surface. This is because rainwater is slightly acidic, and it dissolves the lime in the soil and washes (leaches) it down through the soil. As a result, soils in high rainfall areas are more likely to be acid than alkaline.

Plants that Depend on Acid Soil

Most plants that grow naturally on acid soils (known as calcifuge) usually struggle when grown in anything else. This is because they are unable to take up enough iron from an alkaline soil.

Above: Azaleas are a form of rhododendron, and like them they require an acid soil to survive.

Some excellent garden plants grow only in acid soil, so if your garden has this condition, you can look forward to growing some real treasures.

Acid soils are generally not a problem to plant because in addition to those plants that prefer them, many plants also tolerate them. If your soil is not very acid and your climate isn't too wet, there is little restriction on what you can grow, although it may be wise to avoid Mediterranean plants such as *Cistus* and lavender which thrive in dry alkaline conditions.

Many evergreen shrubs will grow on acid soil. The glossy ovate green leaves of rhododendrons, azaleas, camellias and skimmias provide

Above: *Pieris thrive on acid soil. They are grown for their red-flushed young leaves and cascades of white bell-like flowers.*

wonderful backdrops for their often startlingly bright blooms that provide colour from mid-spring through the early summer. Pieris has the added attraction of red-flushed young leaves.

Permanent foliage plants also include ground covers and creeping plants like gaultherias, heathers and heaths.

Deciduous trees growing on acid soils produce some stunning autumn foliage colour. Outstanding among these are the maples (*Acer*). Many of the spring- and summer-flowering deciduous shrubs also have good autumn colour.

Plenty of perennials and annuals that grow on a wide range of soils can be used to provide seasonal highlights for the border. Wake robin, Himalayan blue poppies and lupins, however, require a slightly acid soil.

Above: *Lupins come in many lovely shades and have a distinctive peppery scent. They require a slightly acid soil.*

Year-round Interest

Acid-loving shrubs are often associated with their stunning spring flowers. The showy white, pink, red or yellow flowers of camellias, rhododendrons and azaleas bloom in abundance and are deservedly much admired. The waxy beauty of magnolia blooms, in cream or blush, is breathtaking. Witch hazels produce their surprisingly frost-resistant and fragrant, spidery blooms, in yellow to dark red, from midwinter to early spring.

Many deciduous shrubs, including maples and witch hazels, are prized for their autumn foliage colour. And there are berries, too. Several species of

Above: Heather (Calluna vulgaris) *needs acid soil to surive. Most varieties flower in late summer and autumn.*

Gaultheria produce white or purple-red fruit at this time. Some shrubs also have attractive bark.

For colour through spring and summer try Wake robin, Himalayan blue poppies and lupins.

Heathers form stunning carpets of flower colour in late summer and autumn. Many varieties are grown for their foliage, which changes colour during the year.

Above: Magnolias make splendid specimen shrubs. Many species need an acid soil.

Above: Spring- and summer-flowering Wake robin (Trillium grandiflorum) *grows well in moist, shaded soil.*

Neutralizing Acid Soil

Adding lime to the soil is an easy and effective way to reduce the acidity. However, it needs to be applied to ground that is bare of plants, dug in and left to break down for several weeks at least, or preferably longer. This is only really practical on vegetable plots, which can be left bare during the winter.

Lime should never be applied at the same time as fertilizer, as the lime will cause the fertilizer to break down too quickly. It can be used when renovating or making a new border, but most ornamental plants tolerate moderately acid soil, so it is not generally worthwhile trying to neutralize acid soil in order to grow acid-hating ornamentals in your garden.

An alternative to liming is to incorporate spent mushroom compost, which is rich in lime. You may even have the benefit of a small crop of mushrooms, as there are often spores in the compost.

PLANTS FOR ACID SOIL

Acer
Amelanchier
Azalea
Calluna vulgaris
Camellia
Erica cultivars
Gaultheria procumbens
Hamamelis
Lupinus
Magnolia
Meconopsis betonicifolia
Pieris
Rhododendron
Skimmia
Trillium grandiflorum

Above: An ornamental border should not need any application of lime for the plants to do well, even on acid soil. This colourful display of established fuchsias and dahlias will tolerate moderately acid conditions.

21

unavailable to lime-hating plants, which then grow poorly as a result and often have yellowing leaves.

Plants that Depend on Alkaline Soil

Some plants can only grow in an alkaline soil, and these are known as calcicole, or lime-loving. They have adapted to cope with the high alkalinity and cannot survive on other types of soil.

Most plants are more tolerant, but many still enjoy alkaline conditions. Among them are many Mediterranean plants, including *Santolina, Artemisia, Helianthemum, Cistus* and herbs, which benefit from the good drainage.

ALKALINE SOIL

These soils are predominantly found in chalky or limestone areas or where there is builder's rubble in the soil. They are free draining with only moderate fertility.

In some areas a shallow layer of soil overlies solid chalk or limestone rock, which can make gardening problematic. The plant roots will have great difficulty penetrating the soft rock, which can lead to poor anchorage, particularly in trees. Also, during dry periods a thin soil can hold only limited reserves of water and the upper levels of the rock become extremely dry.

Once established, however, many plants will produce an extensive, deep root system that penetrates fissures, so that when rain does fall, they can absorb the maximum amount before it drains away.

High alkalinity in soil can cause various nutrient and trace elements to become locked in a form that is

Above: Mediterranean plants, such as Cistus, *thyme and sage, cope well with alkaline conditions.*

Planning Displays

Warm and well-drained chalk and limestone soils play host to a diverse mix of plants, some with more delicate floral attributes than others, but all repaying close inspection.

A host of attractive flowering shrubs tolerate alkaline conditions, such as *Berberis*, *Buddleja davidii*, *Choisya ternata*, *Deutzia*, *Philadelphus*, *Sorbus* and viburnums. Many members of the pea family, including brooms, *Gleditsia* and *Robinia*, often excel on these soils.

Clematis and honeysuckle are useful climbers, the former for their long flowering period and the latter for their intoxicating scent.

Tough perennials like *Acanthus*, *Achillea*, *Eryngium* carnations, *Hypericum* and *Verbascum* are all

Above: Free-flowering mallows (Lavatera) are tolerant of a wide range of soil conditions. They bloom throughout summer.

useful for the middle to back of a border. Wild flowers such as cornflowers and foxgloves can be included. Smaller perennials for the foreground include *Bergenia*, *Doronicum*, scabious and drought-resistant thymes.

Plants with silvery-grey foliage like pinks, saxifrage and *Gypsophila* seem to have a softening effect on a sunny border, and they contribute their own attractive flowers. In shady spots you can plant stinking hellebore, wild orchids, *Iris foetidissima*, *Colchicum* and *Campanula*.

For filling in gaps, there are numerous annuals and biennials, including *Lavatera*, *Matthiola*, *Tagetes* and many everlasting flowers that can be dried in the autumn.

Above: Berberis is a versatile shrub that will tolerate many soil types, including alkaline ones.

23

Year-round Interest

With so many lovely plants thriving on alkaline soil, maintaining interest through the year is not a problem.

There are bulbs that flower in every season, but spring is when most of them produce their jewel-like colour. Spring flowers also come from plants as diverse as *Helleborus orientalis*, peonies, *Doronicum* and lilac. In summer *Helianthemum*, pinks, carnations, *Gypsophila*, *Verbascum* and clematis take over. Lavender and scabious continue well into autumn, when cotoneasters and firethorn flash their red, orange or yellow berries.

The Christmas rose (*Helleborus niger*) reveals its graceful white flowers through winter.

Some deciduous trees grown for autumn foliage are often described as lime-tolerant (typically *Acer davidii* and *A. rubrum*). Yet they do not always produce their foliage display on soils with a high alkaline content.

Instead, the leaves shrivel and fall, so to avoid disappointment it is better not to plant them in alkaline soil. However, *Sorbus sargentiana*, *Euonymus alatus* and *E. europaeus* will produce brilliant autumnal colour, even on poor soils over chalk.

Above: Bulbs are useful for spring colour. Here, massed tulips fill a border in late spring.

Above: French lavender (Lavandula stoechas) *thrives in the free-draining conditions of alkaline soil.*

PLANTS THAT THRIVE IN ALKALINE SOIL
Buddleja davidii
Clematis
Cotoneaster
Dianthus
Doronicum
Gypsophyla paniculata
Helianthemum nummularium
Helleborus
Lavandula
Paeonia
Pyracantha
Scabiosa
Syringa
Verbascum

Correcting Alkaline Conditions

Even though there is a wide range of plants that will tolerate high alkalinity, if you want an even richer diversity of species it will be necessary to improve the organic content of the soil. Adding copious quantities of bulky organic material, such as well-rotted farmyard manure, leaf mould, garden compost and turf, will improve moisture retention and the humus content of the soil. Incorporating organic matter is best done soon after a period of rain.

Adding dried blood and balanced artificial fertilizers can also help to improve the nutrient levels. Chalk soils tend to be lacking in potash, which must be applied for non-lime-loving plants to do well.

Sometimes, breaking up the top 60cm (24in) layer of underlying chalk with a fork or spade will help roots to develop more easily and give plants a good start.

Above: *Adding well-rotted manure, garden compost or leaf mould will improve the soil structure and nutrient content.*

Above: *A prolific clematis scrambles over a wall. It thrives in alkaline conditions as long as its roots are protected from the sun.*

SANDY SOIL

The low clay content in sandy soils (less than 8 per cent) makes them much less water-retentive than clay soils. Their particles are also larger than those of clay, making the soils light, free-draining and relatively infertile.

Sandy soils warm up quickly in spring, so planting out can start early, but they also cool down quickly.

Making the Best of a Sandy Soil

The easiest solution for coping with a sandy soil is to grow only drought-resistant plants that require few nutrients. Many of these originate in dry areas of low fertility, and you will find enough plants to create interesting displays without having to resort to wholesale enrichment of the soil.

Above: Brachyglottis *grows in sites that are too dry for many other plants, but it needs plenty of sunshine.*

Most plants that can cope with a sandy soil are deep-rooted, so that they can seek out moisture at low levels. Cacti and other succulents have fleshy leaves, stems or roots which can store water when it is available for use during dry periods.

Other plants have silvery-grey foliage to reflect sunlight or sparse, small, leathery or spiny leaves to reduce moisture loss through evaporation from the plant. Many of these plants are Mediterranean in origin.

Above: Drought-resistant plants such as thyme are perfect for growing in light sandy soil.

MEDITERRANEAN PLANTS FOR SANDY SOIL

Brachyglottis
Cistus
Helianthemum
Lavender
Origanum
Rosemary
Sage
Santolina
Thyme

Planning Displays

With foliage ranging from spiny yuccas to the soft feathery fronds of tamarisk, you can use all the different foliage shapes, textures and colours to good effect. Many spiny plants have architectural stature around which you can base your planting. Among these are the giant thistle (*Onopordum acanthium*) and the spiky-leaved, metallic-blue flowered *Eryngium*. *Echinops ritro* 'Veitch's Blue' has stunning blue, globular thistle flowers. Silver foliage perfectly sets off the mauve and soft hazy blue flowers that many of these plants produce. Red valerian (*Centranthus ruber*) also combines well with silvers and greys. Or you could try the yellow-green of spurges for an interesting effect.

Above: Yellow-green spurges make an interesting contrast with the silver of Elaeagnus 'Quicksilver' and a deadnettle.

Grasses such as blue fescue (*Festuca glauca*) will add shape and movement. Allow sun-loving ground-covering plants such as *Nepeta* and rock roses to spill over from a border onto paths. In more shaded border edges encourage woodland plants.

Cornfield annuals, which grow on a wide range of soils, are useful for filling in blocks of colour. To create a meadow-like planting, which can be left semi-wild, sow seed in spring or autumn with a good mix of other wild flowers and grasses.

Above: Black-eyed Susan (Rudbeckia) *enjoys free-draining conditions, but do not let the soil dry out completely.*

SUMMER ANNUALS FOR
SANDY SOIL

Calendula officinalis
Centaurea cyanus
Eschscholzia californica
Gypsophila
Lobularia maritima
Papaver rheas Shirley Series
Rudbeckia hirta
Silene alpestris

Year-round Interest

Sea buckthorn provides year-round value. It has narrow silvery leaves and tiny yellow spring flowers, which on female plants are followed in autumn by abundant orange berries. In winter, when many other plants have died, the buckthorn's shapely stems continue to provide interest.

From spring to autumn, silvery foliage provides a perfect backcloth for the bright colours of nearly all the popular summer annuals. Among the perennials, the tall spires of *Acanthus spinosus* carry white flowers and purple bracts from late spring to mid-summer, red valerian blooms from late spring to the end of summer and yellow, pink or white achilleas last all summer long.

Spiny herbaceous plants like thistles, *Eryngium* and *Echinops* can be left standing after they have finished flowering, so that their intricate outlines will continue adding interest.

Above: Eryngium giganteum *thrives in the poorest of soils, as long as they are well drained and in full sun.*

On acid soils, heather flowers in pinks and white from midsummer to autumn. Its foliage comes in many shades of green or golden yellow and often changes colour in winter quite dramatically. Some varieties of heather flower in winter or spring, and these can tolerate alkaline soils.

Above: Like other heathers, crimson-flowered Calluna vulgaris *'Darkness' enjoys sandy soil as long as it is acid.*

PLANTS THAT PREFER SANDY SOIL

Acanthus spinosus
Achillea
Calluna vulgaris
Centranthus ruber
Cistus
Echinops ritro 'Veitch's Blue'
Erica
Eryngium giganteum
Euphorbia
Festuca glauca
Lavatera
Nepeta x *faassenii*
Onopordum acanthium
Papaver orientale
Phormium
Tamarix
Yucca gloriosa

Improving Sandy Soil

Adding plenty of organic matter, such as well-rotted manure, garden compost or leaf mould, will improve sandy soil. Many ornamental garden plants, however, will still need frequent and thorough watering during dry periods, and regular applications of fertilizer to increase the nutrient levels.

Creating Sandy Conditions

You may wish to grow some plants that thrive on sandy soil but find that your soil is too wet, heavy and fertile. In this case, you can create a dry sandy or gravelly garden. It does not need to be very large, but would provide the ideal spot for displaying some attractive plants.

> **GARDENER'S TIP**
> Heather (*Calluna vulgaris*) makes an excellent ground cover for sandy soil that is also acid. The many cultivars allow you to create a permanent carpet in a choice of shades that change according to the season.

Creating an arid-planting area will involve scraping away some of the topsoil to reduce fertility. Mix in enough sharp sand and gravel to improve drainage and create the sort of conditions you need. Adding areas of gravel or pebbles on the surface will add to the impression of a dry landscape.

If drainage is very poor, consider introducing some drainage channels filled with gravel to take away excess water fast.

Above: Potentillas are perfect plants for poor, free-draining soils. Alpine types prefer a gritty, sharply draining soil.

Above: Evening primrose and daisy-like feverfew both enjoy a sunny position on sandy soil.

29

Left: Yellow-flowering Berberis linearifolia *will thrive in most soils, but will benefit from improved drainage on very heavy ones.*

growth, making them very fertile. Plants growing in clay soil suffer less from the effects of drought in all but the driest of summers.

Clay soils can be acid, neutral or alkaline, which will also affect your choice of plants. Generally, however, the clay content of soil is a more important factor than its acidity or alkalinity in determining which plants will do well.

Clay Soil

This type of soil will consist of more than 25 per cent clay particles, which makes it moisture-retentive, heavy and sticky. It may become waterlogged in wet weather, is slow to warm up in spring, and may bake hard in summer.

Really heavy, sticky clay soils are unworkable when wet and easily compacted and must not be walked on.

Due to their moisture retention, however, clay soils also hold on to nutrients that plants need for healthy

Making the Best of Clay Soil

Grow plants with a vigorous constitution, as those are the ones likely to do best. Plants need to be resilient enough to withstand wet soil in winter

Above: Pyracantha *makes an impenetrable barrier when grown as an informal garden hedge.*

GARDENER'S TIP

Physically working clay soil is largely a matter of timing. If you try to do it when it is too wet it will form an impenetrable layer at the depth you dig down to, for plant roots and draining water alike. Leave it until it is too dry and you will be working with what feels like lumps of rock.

Left: The delightfully scented Rosa *'Zéphirine Drouhin' is thornless and is an excellent climber.*

enriched you can achieve a more or less traditional scheme with roses and herbaceous underplanting.

Generally, those reliable herbaceous perennials that tolerate a heavy clay soil are also plants that grow well in moist marginal, waterside plantings, such as *Astilbe, Mimulus, Phormium, Hosta, Houttuynia, Lysimachia, Gunnera* and *Rodgersia*. These provide plenty of striking architectural foliage and some arresting blooms.

It is possible to grow some bulbs in clay soil, but they will not survive if the soil becomes waterlogged during wet periods. Planting them on a layer of grit will help.

without rotting. But in the summer, they can take advantage of the soil's moisture-retaining properties, even when the surface is baked hard.

Planning Displays

Several resilient shrubs grow well on clay. Choose those that offer spring or summer flowers, autumn foliage or berries, or attractive coloured stems for the winter months.

Roses, too, are more tolerant of clay than many plants, and in a border that has been well prepared and

---

SHRUBS FOR CLAY SOIL

Berberis
Cornus
Cotoneaster
Crataegus
Philadelphus
Pyracantha
Viburnum opulus

Above: Hostas thrive in moist soils, and in time they will spread to form a large, domed clump.

mock orange. *Berberis* produces bright yellow flowers in spring, and berries in autumn, adding to the colourful yellow, orange or red berries of *Cotoneaster* and *Pyracantha*. Guelder rose also has fleshy red berries and crabs have their apples.

In winter the coloured stems of dogwood and the contorted twigs of *Salix babylonica* var. *pekinensis* 'Tortuoasa' are visually arresting. Small willows are covered with silver catkins if you cut them back hard each spring to produce masses of new growth.

Year-round Interest

As there is such a variety of plants that you can grow on all but the heaviest of clay soils, planting for interest through the year should not be a problem.

Small trees and shrubs have much to offer. The blossom of cherries, crab apples and hawthorn in spring is followed by that of guelder rose and

---

PLANTS THAT THRIVE ON
CLAY SOIL

Astilbe
Caltha palustris
Crambe cordifolia
Gunnera manicata
Hosta
Papaver somniferum
Philadelphus
Primula vulgaris
Rheum
Rodgersia
Rosa
Trollius

Above: The white flowers of Crambe cordifolia *create an ethereal haze when planted in a large group.*

Large-growing leafy perennials like *Gunnera*, *Rheum*, the giant thistles and *Crambe cordifolia* grow especially well on clay, usually to dramatic proportions.

Among flowering perennials yellow primroses and cowslips are soon followed by meadow flowers such as burnets and cranesbills. A host of summer flowers includes hollyhocks, *Mimulus*, *Phlox* and foxgloves.

Improving Clay Soil

The best way to improve clay soil is to add plenty of organic matter in early autumn or late spring, when the soil is workable. This will open up the soil and make it more balanced, allowing

Above: Roses like the moist fertility of clay soils, particularly when plenty of organic matter is added.

Above: Primroses (Primula vulgaris) are ideal for a cottage garden or mossy bank, as long as the soil remains moist.

nutrients and moisture to be readily absorbed by plant roots. It will also improve drainage and make the soil more workable when digging is required. Applications of fertilizer will also be more effective.

Where waterlogged soil is a problem, you can try growing bog-loving plants, or improve the drainage – either by digging in grit or, more expensively, installing drainage channels filled with shingle.

Clay soils can be quite acid, especially when they are waterlogged and moss grows on the surface. If you are making a new border it may be worth altering the pH level. You can do this by adding lime as described in the section on Acid Soils.

Planting in Different Locations

THE ASPECT OF A PLOT, THE AMOUNT OF SHELTER IT HAS, THE DEGREE OF SHADE OR SUN IT RECEIVES AND THE MOISTURE CONTENT OF THE SOIL ARE ALL RELEVANT WHEN CHOOSING PLANTS THAT WILL THRIVE OVER A LONG PERIOD.

ASPECT

The direction your garden or border faces and its relationship to your house or adjacent buildings will influence the environment your plants will be growing in. As the sun moves around the house, different areas of the garden can be thrown into shade or receive the full glare of the sun for various amounts of time. Shade can be full, partial or dappled. In winter a deeply shaded position can be very damp and cold, whereas in summer it can be pleasant. The sun can at times be far too hot in summer, but of great benefit during short cold days. And as the seasons change, your garden may be subjected to frost and bitter winds.

Above: Clematis montana *will grow happily on an east-facing wall which gives it some protection.*

All these factors should be considered before planting, as they will have a bearing on which plants will do well in different parts of the garden.

Heavily Shaded Gardens

Some gardens may have shade from the house for long stretches of the day. In winter deep shade will make the garden cold and damp. The winter cold will be aggravated if the garden is also exposed to strong, cold winds, so a sheltering hedge may help, but in spite of these disadvantages, there are plants that not only tolerate these conditions but actually prefer them.

Above: Sweet-smelling Mexican orange-blossom (Choisya ternata) *can survive conditions in a shaded, cold garden.*

East-facing Gardens

An east wind in winter is the cruellest and when combined with a frost can spell instant death to plants that are less than hardy, and will nip tender buds. As with a shaded garden, a fence or hedge on the boundary will give some protection. However, a garden with a predominantly easterly aspect has the benefit of morning and early afternoon sun.

Gardens in Full Sun

The most sought-after aspect for most gardeners is a sunny one. With a house providing shelter against cold winds and a garden that takes full advantage of the sun's warming rays throughout the year it seems like an ideal location. At the height of summer, however, the sun can be relentlessly hot and glaring and will quickly dry out thin soil.

Some form of shading, perhaps attractive fences, screens of climbers, tall shrubs or small trees will be welcomed by many plants, as well as humans.

Sunny gardens are ideal for growing hot-climate and sun-loving plants, and exotic tender and half-hardy plants will thrive and even last well into the autumn if the garden is protected from wind.

West-facing Gardens

These gardens are likely to have some shade through the mornings, until the sun swings round at its highest point. But they then benefit for the rest of the day and in summer this can be quite late, when the low rays intensify colours. These are also warm gardens, unless they catch some of the colder winds, so you will need to assess whether some protection is needed.

Above: Blue Agapanthus *share a sunny border with vibrantly coloured summer bulbs such as lilies and* Crocosmia.

PLANTS FOR HEAVILY SHADED POSITIONS

Berberis x *stenophylla*
Camellia japonica
Clematis alpina
Choisya ternata
Garrya elliptica
Hydrangea petiolaris
Ilex corallina
Jasminum nudiflorum
Mahonia japonica

PLANTS FOR EAST-FACING POSITIONS

Bergenia cordifolia
Chaenomeles x *superba*
Cotoneaster horizontalis
Euphorbia griffithii
Hamamelis mollis
Helleborus feotidus
Lonicera periclymenum
Rosa rugosa
Vinca major

PLANTS FOR SUNNY POSITIONS

Agapanthus
Canna indica
Eccremocarpus scaber
Echinacea purpurea
Echinops ritro
Helenium
Kniphofia
Lilium lancifolium
Osteospermum
Yucca filamentosa
Zauschneria californica

PLANTS FOR WEST-FACING POSITIONS

Ceanothus
Crocosmia cultivars
Geranium 'Johnson's Blue'
Humulus lupulus 'Aureus'
Papaver orientale
Penstemon cultivars
Vitis coignetiae

Selecting Suitable Plants for Different Aspects

Before growing any new plants in your garden it is wise to establish that they will be suitable for the situation you intend them to occupy. A good local nursery will give advice on the best plants for your locality and particular situation.

Make sure, also, that you select a few plants to give some colour or interest for each season. Even if your garden faces predominantly east or is shady and cold, there should be several plants that will give pleasure even in the depths of winter.

Above: *A smoke bush* (Cotinus) *has been planted so that the evening sun shines through its purple foliage.*

WINDY SITES

Gusting wind can spoil plants in exposed areas. Light plants are at risk of being blown over. Plants with soft, tender foliage are likely to be scorched by the wind resulting in brown, withered leaves and poor growth.

Creating a windbreak will minimize the problem. One that is partly permeable to the wind is much more effective than a solid one, which can cause localized turbulence where the wind is deflected. Black windbreak netting is efficient but unsightly; depending on where you want to put it you could disguise it with trellis. A trellis clothed with climbers would slow down much of the wind, even without netting. Where there is sufficient room, a

Above: Spiraea japonica *is a tough shrub that can withstand strong wind. This one is* 'Goldflame'.

screen of tall, wind-tolerant shrubs planted along the most vulnerable side will be very effective. Many plants will tolerate this kind of exposure while providing colour and interest throughout the year. A broken windbreak would allow a good view to continue to be appreciated.

Staking vulnerable plants will also help protect them in windy areas.

Above: Helleborus orientalis *tolerates most conditions but needs shelter from strong, cold winds.*

WIND-TOLERANT PLANTS

Cornus alba 'Aurea'
Cotinus coggygria
Euonymus fortunei cultivars
Hamamelis virginiana
Hippophäe rhamnoides
Hydrangea paniculata
'Grandiflora'
Lavatera olbia
Lonicera pileata
Mahonia aquifolium
Philadelphus 'Belle Etoile'
Spiraea japonica
Tamarix tetrandra
Taxus baccata
Thuja occidentalis

SHADY MOIST SITES

Some people might regard the presence of a permanently shaded damp patch in their garden as a real problem, because many plants cannot cope with dark, wet conditions. Most bulbs, for instance, dislike very wet soil and will simply rot if waterlogged. Many ordinary garden plants will also die in persistently wet conditions.

It is these very conditions, however, that account for the lush and often large foliage of moisture-loving plants. Big leaves are nature's way of ensuring that the maximum amount of chlorophyll is exposed to the limited light to help photosynthesis (food manufacture) by the plant.

Above: Grow lily-of-the-valley (Convallaria majalis) *in full or partial shade in a moist location.*

Making the Best of a Shady Moist Site

The best way of coping with the area is to stop regarding it as a problem and see it as a wonderful opportunity for growing some lovely plants that would be unhappy in a drier situation.

Wetland plants have distinct preferences for the different types of wet site, so you need to match the plants to the conditions of your site. Most simply prefer permanently moist soil. Some plants can cope with particularly wet sites that are virtually permanently boggy and occasionally waterlogged. Similarly, some plants can grow in dappled or deep shade. Some, of course, can cope with all types of shade.

Above: Rhododendrons are available in a wide variety of colours. They need an acid soil and a position out of hot sunlight.

Above: A dense planting of different types of hosta keeps weeds at bay in a moist shady border.

Planning Displays

Make the most of the great variety of luxuriant foliage produced by shade- and moisture-loving plants. You can contrast the different types, colours and forms of foliage to make an interesting green tapestry of leaves. For example, place tall, strappy irises next to soft feathery ferns or the big pleated leaves of *Veratrum*.

If you work with a wide selection of different foliage forms and colours, you can create a planting that has as much interest as a colourful sunny flower border. And if you include a few evergreen shrubs as well, such as aucubas, skimmias, mahonias and fatsias, the display will last throughout the growing season, and into winter. All these shrubs have the added bonus of beautiful spring flowers, many of which are followed by colourful fruits. For foliage at ground level be sure to include hostas, bergenias and ivies.

Make the most of those perennial plants that flower in moist shade by placing them as occasional colourful highlights against the lush green foliage. The yellow spires of *Ligularia*, for instance, show up splendidly against a green backdrop. Where the planting edges are in dappled or partial shade, you have the opportunity to include more brightly coloured woodland plants than would grow in the darker shade.

Above: Delicate yellow flowers of Alchemilla mollis *contrast with lacy fern fronds in a shady damp corner.*

39

Left: Winter aconites (Eranthis hyemalis) *come through the soil before much else is stirring on the woodland floor.*

Woodland plants provide some real treasures in spring: winter aconites, primroses, snowdrops, snake's-head fritillaries and wake robin followed by lily-of-the-valley and wood anemones. Dicentras produce arching sprays of pendulous pink or white flowers.

Summer highlights are provided by many shade-loving perennials such as delicate *Astilbe, Astrantia major* and *Ligularia. Meconopsis cambrica, Impatiens* and pansies have long-flowering seasons. Rodgersia flowers in pinks, reds and white. The blues of monkshood (*Aconitum*) are useful from midsummer to autumn.

Helleborus niger and *H. orientale* produce white or greenish cream blooms through winter to spring. Witch hazels and sarcococcas also produce fragrant flowers in winter, in yellow and white respectively.

Year-round Interest

Even in a shady, damp spot you can guarantee some colour and interest for every season.

Aucubas have glossy green leaves and bear small red-purple flowers in mid-spring, which on female plants are followed by bright red berries in autumn. Variegated leaf forms are better in dappled shade. The scented spring flowers of skimmias are pink in bud opening to creamy white and followed by green berries usually ripening to red. The yellowish-green autumn flowers of mature ivies are followed by small black fruit, which are a good source of food for birds.

For dappled shade *Fatsia japonica* has big, glossy hand-shaped leaves. In partial shade evergreen mahonias have scented yellow spring flowers followed by blue to black berries. Rhododendrons and camellias both have showy spring blooms. *Viburnum davidii* bears tiny white flowers at this time, and on female plants these give way to turquoise fruits.

Above: The delightful flowers of Astrantia major *brighten up lightly shaded corners in summer.*

Creating Shady Damp Conditions

Even if your garden is not naturally wet, you can take advantage of a shady area to create a damp spot. Dig out a hollow, line it with black butyl liner with some drainage holes punched through, then return the soil, mixed with plenty of organic matter. The liner will act like a layer of natural clay, helping to hold the moisture in the soil and reducing the need for watering.

However, if you do create an artificially moist site, you will have to be prepared to keep the soil moist by watering in periods of drought.

Above: The delicate flowers of dicentras *thrive in a partially shaded border. They prefer neutral to alkaline soil.*

PLANTS THAT THRIVE IN
MOIST SHADE
Astilbe hybrids
Astrantia
Dicentra
Eranthis hyemalis
Fatsia japonica
Hamamelis mollis
Helleborus
Hosta
Rhododendron
Rodgersia
Sarcococca
Viburnum davidii

Above: Rodgersias *enjoy a waterside location. They grow in full sun as well as partial shade, rather than full shade.*

SUNNY MOIST SITES

Areas around natural ponds and streams can be damp or wet, and they tend to be open and sunny. The margins of a pond are waterlogged, which means that only plants adapted to have their roots permanently or seasonally in water will survive there. The dampness of the soil decreases the further away from the pond it is. A different range of plants are adapted to each level of dampness, and there is no shortage of plants that love these type of conditions.

Making the Best of a Sunny Moist Site

The moist areas around a pond or along a stream are the ideal place to create a lush garden. Wetland foliage plants tend to be vigorous, often

> ### PLANTS FOR SUNNY MOIST SITES
>
> *Caltha palustris*
> *Cornus alba*
> *Darmera peltata*
> *Filipendula*
> *Gunnera*
> *Iris sibirica*
> *Ligularia*
> *Lysimachia nummularia* 'Aurea'
> *Lysichiton*
> *Primula bullyeana*
> *Primula denticulata*
> *Rheum*
> *Ranunculus ficaria*
> *Rodgersia*
> *Trollius*
> *Salix*
> *Zantedeschia aethiopica*

growing to giant proportions in summer. Even in lower temperatures all the foliage plants seem to double in size daily. This is splendid for large areas, but if you only have a small site you may have to forgo the large plants and use smaller ones instead.

The water's edge provides the opportunity for growing some exquisitely flowered marginal plants. The plants must be able to cope with extremely wet conditions, and at certain times of the year to grow in water. Marginal plants create a perfect transition between the exuberant foliage on firm land and the special qualities of water.

Left: Gunnera manicata *produces some of the largest leaves seen in gardens, up to 2m (6ft) long on stalks that can be 2.5m (8ft) long.*

Planning Displays

A sunny damp garden or area is an excellent opportunity to grow some exciting large perennial foliage plants such as gunneras, rodgersias and rheums, which also thrive in more shady conditions, but they need plenty of space. In a small area, you can still create an impressive effect with the lush foliage of hostas, with the added bonus of their delicate flowers in summer. Ligularias, irises and astibles also flower well in these conditions.

Position the tallest plants either at the rear or in the centre of a moist plot, where they will not hide smaller plants. Smaller growing plants can then be planted in front of them.

Plenty of smaller perennials bear delicate, exquisitely coloured blooms above their lush, spreading foliage.

Above: The red, jagged foliage of the ornamental rhubarb, Rheum *'Ace of Hearts', is spectacular.*

*Above: Creeping Jenny (*Lysimachia nummularia *'Aurea') works well as a ground cover, as long as all perennial weeds have been removed first.*

The bright yellows of marsh marigolds, lesser celandines and globe-flowers are counter-balanced by the hazy blues of water forget-me-nots, purple loosestrife and creamy meadow-sweet creating a country cottage effect. Many primulas come in an exciting range of colours and are invaluable for smaller settings. Once established they will spread quickly.

For permanent structure, dwarf Japanese maples and small weeping willows work well. Many have stunning autumn foliage, and some also have colourful bark that looks good in winter. Avoid larger willows as these would soon grow to a huge size, and their roots are extensive.

Year-round Interest

With large lush foliage and flower stems reaching for the sky, plants that thrive in the damp, sunny site make a dense and luxuriant effect from spring through to late autumn. Spring and early summer are perhaps the very best seasons, but careful inclusion of certain plants will guarantee colour later on as well.

Flower colour is available from spring to autumn, starting with the golden-yellow flowers of the marsh marigolds. *Lysichiton americanum* produces bright yellow flowers in spring. Purple drumstick primulas (*Primula denticulata*) flower in late spring, and *P. bulleyana* contributes hot colours in early summer, followed by the arum lily with its elegant white blooms.

Above: The arum lily (Zantedeschia aethiopica) *is perfect for a waterside planting. It will also grow in shallow water.*

Above: In a moist corner under dappled shade, primulas, forget-me-nots, columbines and bluebells celebrate the arrival of spring.

Perennial foliage plants last from spring to summer, but the giant leaves of *Darmera peltata* will turn red in autumn before they disappear. This plant also bears white to bright pink flowers on 2m (6ft) long stems in late spring. Do include rodgersias: their leaves turn bronze and red in autumn and their white or pink fluffy flowers are followed by dark red fruits.

Evergreen foliage plants provide year-round interest. Include *Bergenia* for edging and enjoy the added bonus of their pink blooms early in the year.

For a splash of winter colour, the bare red stems of *Cornus alba* cannot be beaten. Cut these hard back every spring to guarantee plenty of new stems. Different cultivars have variously coloured autumn leaves.

Maintaining Sunny Moist Conditions

The foliage of the vigorous plants makes excellent ground cover, which helps to conserve moisture. But even a naturally moist area may dry out during hot dry summers, as do many natural watercourses. You may need to water the area to maintain the moistness that the plants require.

Avoid planting tall trees that could eventually overshadow the site. If nearby plants threaten to encroach the area, you will have to prune them carefully to maintain their distance.

Creating a Moist Area

If you want to grow moisture-loving plants but you don't have a suitable site, you can create a damp patch quite easily by digging out soil to make a

Above: This lush summer border has been planted with a delightful combination of fresh yellows and greens.

hollow and lining it with butyl pond liner. Mix plenty of organic matter into the soil and return it to the hollow.

If you are making a pond, it is a good idea to run the liner under the soil some way from the margin of the pond in order to create a damp area. Garden ponds do not have to be large, and even a 1 x 1m (3 x 3ft) pond, with a butyl liner, will provide the correct environment for a good selection of water-loving plants. If you make the pond with more than one level, with a gradual slope towards the edge, you can grow a wide range of aquatic and marginal plants, as well as attracting a host of wildlife.

Left: The fresh, bright colours of these marginal plants create an attractive naturalistic arrangement.

SUNNY DRY SITES

Most gardens have patches where there is less moisture than elsewhere. "Rain shadows" caused by buildings or other structures, shallow or rocky soil, or disturbed sandy or gravelly subsoil can all cause dry conditions. Any of these situations combined with full sun will render any attempts to wet the soil artificially unsuccessful. Sunny gardens or borders set against a wall or next to a patio are particularly likely to be hot and dry.

On the positive side, dry soils are quick to warm up in spring, allowing you to plant out earlier than in many other sites. But you will need to keep young plants well watered.

Above: Rosemary does particularly well in a dry, sunny location as it is native to the Mediterranean.

Making the Best of a Sunny Site

A sunny dry site does not need to be a problem if you select plants that appreciate such an environment. Mediterranean plants are an obvious choice. Lavender, rosemary, sage, salvia, santolina, rock roses (*Cistus*), helichrysum and marigolds are just some of the plants that like a position in full sun and dry soil.

These plants have evolved and adapted to cope with high temperatures, low rainfall and often with poor soil. These adaptations, which include silvery, downy and sometimes succulent foliage, are often what make the plants so attractive and useful in displays for the inside as well as outside.

Above: The evergreen leaves of sage provide fragrance all year round, and they are useful in the kitchen.

Above: Geranium *'Johnson's Blue'* produces masses of veined purple-blue flowers during the summer.

Planning Displays

A dry planting in full sun works particularly well if it is planned with a feel for a naturally dry landscape. You can even create a dry-gravel river bed effect that will set off the drought-resistant plants beautifully. Group the plants together to make islands of flowing colour rising out of the gravel. Decide where the architectural plants will go first, then fill in with smaller plants, to make pleasing associations.

Try to blend or contrast flower colours with the foliage. Silver and grey associate well with the purples, blues and mauves that are so common among Mediterranean plants. For contrast with the silvers try the darker green foliage of rock roses. Or use the very hot colours sparingly as eye-catchers.

Be sure to include some aromatic plants that will release their fragrances in hot sun. Mediterranean herbs are highly fragrant. Plant them where you will brush against the leaves as you walk past to release their heady aromas.

You can include grasses, too. They grow in mounds, create interesting backgrounds for borders and add movement and sound as their leaves rustle in a breeze. If you combine a variety of species you can create a stunning effect of shape, texture and colour.

Above: Grasses add form, colour and movement to a display, and they are easy to manage.

47

Year-round Interest

When deciding which plants to use, plan for a succession of interest, with foliage, flowers and then seedheads. Grasses are invaluable, providing interest for most of the year; from summer onwards their tall flowerheads will move gently in the wind.

Year-round foliage plants include spurges, especially *Euphorbia characias* and *E. myrsinites*, which have succulent grey-green or blue-green leaves respectively and flowers with yellow-green bracts from spring to early or midsummer. Rosemary can be grown through mild winters.

Spring is something of a famine for arid-area flowers, but some crocuses, especially the hybrids, prefer well-drained and poor soil conditions, so are worth trying, as are tulips later in the season. *Convulvus cneorum*, a leafy silvery-green evergreen, bears its funnel-shaped white flowers from late spring to summer.

For summer colour there is a wide choice. Cranesbills flower prolifically. *Lavatera* 'Barnsley' has masses of funnel-shaped white flowers ageing to soft pink throughout summer, up to 2m (6ft) high. Some types of allium do well in dry areas, and they flower profusely in summer in shades of pink, purple and white.

From late summer to early autumn, the blue and purple-blue flowers of the shrub *Caryopteris clandonensis* show prettily against its grey-green leaves. Sedums flower at this time, too, in bright pinks and ruby-reds, and are irresistible to bees.

Leave interesting seedheads after flowering to prolong the plant's features. Grey cardoons for instance develop large heads after their thistle-like, purple summer flowers are faded.

Left: The graceful plumes of Cortaderia selloana *last through the winter. The plant looks best in a prime position where it can be seen in its full glory. Cut down completely when the fronds are past their best in early spring to encourage fresh growth.*

Improving a Sunny Dry Site

Although it is usually best to accept the existing conditions and grow drought-tolerant plants, you can take some measures to increase moisture and nutrient levels in the soil. Adding garden compost or leaf mould in the autumn will help.

A mulch such as composted bark in summer will reduce evaporation and suppress weeds, or you can use a permanent mulch of gravel or pebbles, which also provide a beautiful backdrop for the plants.

Creating a Dry Planting Area

It is possible to create a dry area where you can display and enjoy plants from hot, arid areas. Choose a site that receives plenty of sunlight, and preferably one that is sheltered. You will need to scrape away some of the topsoil and use it elsewhere. In wet

Above: Massing plants together can create a lush effect in a hot, dry courtyard.

climates, digging in channels of grit will improve the drainage, allowing the soil to dry out more quickly than it normally would.

A sunny patio with planting spaces between the paving stones is an ideal setting as the area will retain heat well, especially if close to the house. Or you could build a raised bed and fill it with a fast-draining mix that could include gravel or grit.

Above: The round heads of Allium christophii *appear in early summer. Here, they are accompanied by longer flowering* Linaria purpurea.

PLANTS THAT THRIVE IN
A SUNNY DRY SITE

Brachyglottis (syn. *Senecio*)
Calendula
Caryopteris clandonensis
Echinops ritro
Eryngium bourgatii
Euphorbia
Geranium
Helichrysum
Iris germanica hybrids
Kniphofia hybrids
Lavandula
Lavatera
Santolina chamaecyparissus
Sedum

Above: Ivy grows well in dry shady sites, particularly against a wall, but the variegated types do like some sun.

SHADY DRY SITES

Areas beneath a tree canopy or under a wall, fence or hedge often lack moisture. Trees take up an enormous amount of water from the soil, often leaving it dry. Walls and fences can interrupt driving rain, making one side drier than the other. Hedges combine both these drawbacks by interrupting rainfall and taking up moisture from the surrounding ground.

Shade can be deep, with no sun at all, or it can be partial, with some sunlight falling on the site at certain times of day. Dappled shade occurs when sunlight is filtered by leaves and branches. Some shade plants prefer particular types of shade, others can cope with a range.

Making the Best of a Shady Dry Site

This is one of the most difficult sites to contend with, but a few well chosen plants can transform even the most unpromising of areas. Most plants that cope well with dry shade are those that naturally grow in the shadow of other vegetation.

Busy Lizzies are among the very few flowering annuals that will survive in shade, but they do prefer to be kept moist if possible. Many plants that are more naturally found growing in moist shade will tolerate dry shade conditions. These include foxgloves, *Aquilegia*, hellebores and the tall *Acanthus mollis*.

Ivies cope extremely well with dry shade, including deep shade. There are many varieties, with a whole range of different leaf formations that will grow in even the deepest shade. Variegated ivies require some light to colour well.

Above: The spurred violet, blue, pink or white flowers of granny's bonnet (Aquilegia) *will tolerate a dry shady site.*

Planning Displays

Heavily shaded areas will not support a bright array of flower plants, so dry shade plantings have to rely heavily on structure and foliage. Various ever-green shrubs, such as skimmias, hollies and mahonias, can cope with a certain amount of dryness in the soil. Aucubas are invaluable for deep shade, but the variegated varieties, with beautifully yellow-mottled leaves, prefer partial shade.

Try to create contrasts in leaf colour, texture and shape. The glossy prickly leaves of hollies and mahonias, for instance, can be placed against the smooth-edged leaves of other plants. *Iris foetidissima* has long strappy leaves and seems happy in the darkest of spots.

Above: Geranium macrorrhizum *produces abundant flowers even in shade, and will spread to cover a large area.*

Ivies are unbeatable for clothing fences and walls in a variety of leaf shapes and colours. They can also be used for ground cover, as can peri-winkles. Epimediums can also be grown as ground cover under trees and shrubs, where their dainty yellow, white, pink, red or purple flowers provide welcome colour.

In lightly shaded areas, resilient perennials such as monkshood, sweet violet, and some of the cranesbills are good for providing patches of colour against the green foliage.

Above: A shady area with dappled light is the romantic setting for this combination of foliage plants.

GARDENER'S TIP

Dry shady sites are the most difficult to bring bright colour into. One solution is to introduce containers of seasonal plants in flower. These will have benefited from growing in better conditions and will be able to survive a few weeks of gloom. When they finish flowering return them to a brighter situation to recover.

Year-round Interest

Plantings in shade rely heavily on evergreen foliage plants for interest, but a number of these also produce flowers, as do many of the foliage perennials.

The yellow spring flowers of mahonias make a wonderful contrast with their glossy green foliage, and some have the bonus of being scented. Many perennials also flower in spring providing earlier colour. Pink flowers brighten up bergenias, and *Brunnera macrophylla* has blue forget-me-not-like flowers. Where it is not too dry epimediums provide a wide range of colour from spring to early summer. Periwinkles will be scattered with a carpet of violet-blue from spring to autumn.

As summer approaches, more perennial flowers appear. *Anemone x*

Above: The bright berries of a small skimmia planted among bluebells create a startling contrast.

Above: Helleborus foetidus *prefers a site with dappled shade and a neutral to alkaline soil.*

hybrida has pink or white flowers in late summer and autumn, which is when *Liriope muscari* produces spikes packed with blue, bead-like flowers, while monkshood supports spires of blue flowers.

Autumn is the time for a superb display of berries, which can appear on aucuba and hollies, both bright red. Some skimmias bear red, black or white berries after their dainty white flowers. The large seed capsules of *Iris foetidissima* split open at this time of year to display yellow seeds. Through winter and early spring hardy cyclamen planted under trees produce their bright pink flowers and often patterned leaves. *Helleborus foetidus* has nodding bell-shaped green flowers. The scented blue or white flowers of sweet violet see winter out.

Above: Carpet-forming Anemone blanda *will tolerate partial shade. Its flowers appear in spring.*

Improving Shady Dry Conditions

You can alter the level of shade in parts of the garden. If you have a large tree, for example, removing the lower branches allows more light to reach the ground beneath. The branches in the main canopy can also be thinned to create a dappled light. In a dark, sunless area, a fence or wall opposite the site can be painted white to reflect the available light towards the shaded bed or border.

Artificially watering a dry site will help to moisten it, but to maximize the effect, improve the soil by mixing in plenty of organic matter. Adding a mulch to the surface will impede evaporation. Many shade-loving perennials are naturally woodland plants, and so need a woodland-like soil. This should be high in organic matter.

An alternative approach, easier than trying to change the conditions, is to bring in containers temporarily, with flowering or brightly variegated plants to add interest and colour.

PLANTS THAT TOLERATE
DRY SHADE

Aconitum
Anemone x hybrida
Aquilegia
Aucuba japonica
Bergenia
Digitalis purpurea
Helleborus foetidus
Epimedium
Euphorbia
Hedera
Iris foetidissima
Liriope muscari
Mahonia
Skimmia
Vinca

Above: Imported potted plants can bring temporary colour to dry and shady parts of the garden. They can be returned to more suitable areas to recover.

AIRBORNE POLLUTION

Pollution can be a problem for plants in busy urban areas, especially in small front gardens. Deposits from vehicle exhausts settle on foliage throughout the year, and if the road is salted in winter the salt is splashed by cars on to the nearest plants as the traffic passes. Some plants are more tolerant of airborne pollution than others so it is worth knowing which these are if you live near a road, where traffic is constantly streaming past or snarled up in slow-moving jams.

The solution may be as simple as a hedge of plants that can tolerate this kind of treatment along the most vulnerable part of the garden. Such a

Above: Olearia *x* haastii *will produce a mass of snowy white blossoms, even in a polluted atmosphere.*

barrier would protect more delicate species behind it. Good hedging plants are *Berberis*, *Cotoneaster*, holly and privet. But if a hedge is not practical, you may need to concentrate on growing plants that are tolerant of these unfavourable conditions.

Pollution-tolerant Plants with Year-round Interest

A number of pollution-resistant evergreen and deciduous shrubs provide flowers and interesting foliage for the whole year.

Many of the evergreen shrubs have handsome glossy, leathery, dark green leaves, but there are also variegated varieties such as the spotted laurel to

Above: Privet *(*Ligustrum lucidum *'Excelsum Superbum') makes a colourful and useful hedge beside a busy road to act as a barrier that will protect the garden.*

Above: *Silver-leaved* Elaeagnus *'Quicksilver' provides year-round colour and is a useful windbreak.*

PLANTS THAT TOLERATE
POLLUTED AIR

Aucuba japonica
Aquilegia vulgaris
Berberis
Bergenia cordifolia
Cotoneaster
Elaeagnus
Fatsia japonica
Forsythia
Garrya elliptica
Geranium endressii
Helleborus niger
Helleborus orientalis
Hemerocallis
Hosta
Ilex aquifolium
Iris
Lamium
Ligustrum
Olearia x *haastii*
Philadelphus
Pulmonaria
Rudbeckia
Symphytum
Viburnum
Weigela florida

provide extra interest. Some of the deciduous shrubs, including many of the viburnums, end their year with a flourish of vivid autumn colour. Many also produce beautiful spring, summer or even autumn flowers; the summer flowers of *Philadelphus* are delightfully fragrant. For autumn and winter, holly berries are hard to beat and from midwinter to early spring pretty catkins hang from the branches of garryas, which also make useful and effective windbreaks.

The great variety of cotoneasters makes them especially useful as ground cover, for growing up walls or hedging. Different types will bear white to deep pink flowers from spring to summer, most with autumn berries.

In addition to shrubs, there are some virtually indestructible perennials, such as *Bergenia* and *Pulmonaria*.

Above: *Perennial lungwort* (Pulmonaria) *makes good ground cover in shade and can withstand the effects of car fumes.*

Plants for Your Garden

USE THIS LIST OF PLANTS DESCRIBING THEIR IDEAL CONDITIONS AND
SEASON OF INTEREST TO PLAN YOUR GARDEN DESIGN.

Plants	Sow	Plant Out	Season of Interest
Acanthus spinosus (s)	spring	autumn	spring to midsummer
Acer (s)	n/a	autumn	autumn foliage
Achillea (s)	spring, in situ	n/a	summer, autumn
Aconitum (ps, s)	spring	autumn, spring	summer
Amelanchier * (s, ps)	n/a	autumn	spring, autumn
Alcea rosea (s)	summer, in situ	n/a	early to midsummer
Alchemilla (s, ps)	spring	early summer	summer
Allium (s)	n/a	autumn	summer
Anemone x *hybrida* (s, ps)	n/a	divide in spring	late summer to mid-autumn
Anemone nemorosa (ps)	n/a	divide in spring	spring to early summer
Aquilegia (s, ps)	spring	autumn, spring	late spring, early summer
Aruncus (fs, ps)	autumn, spring	autumn, spring	summer
Astilbe (s)	n/a	divide in winter	summer
Astrantia major (s, ps)	autumn	spring	summer
Aucuba japonica (s, ps, fs)	n/a	autumn	year-round
Azalea * (ps)	n/a	autumn	spring
Berberis (s, ps)	n/a	autumn	spring, autumn
Bergenia (s, ps)	n/a	divide in autumn	spring
Brachyglottis (syn. *Senecio*) (s)	n/a	autumn, spring	year-round
Brunnera macrophylla (ps)	spring	autumn, spring	spring
Buddleja davidii (s)	n/a	autumn, spring	summer
Calendula officinalis (s, ps)	spring, in situ	n/a	summer to autumn
Calluna vulgaris * (s)	n/a	autumn, spring	summer, autumn

Achillea

Anemone ranunculoides

Plants	Sow	Plant Out	Season of Interest
Caltha palustris (s)	n/a	spring	spring
Camellia * (ps)	n/a	autumn	spring
Campanula 'G.F. Wilson' (s, ps)	spring	autumn	summer
Canna indica (s)	spring, autumn	early summer	summer, autumn
Caryopteris x *clandonensis* (s)	n/a	autumn, spring	summer. early autumn
Ceanothus (s)	n/a	autumn, spring	late spring
Centaurea cyanus (s)	spring, in situ	n/a	spring to midsummer
Centranthus ruber ^ (s)	spring	autumn	late spring, summer
Chaenomeles x *superba* (s, ps)	n/a	autumn, spring	spring
Choisya ternata (s)	n/a	autumn, spring	late spring, autumn
Cistus (s)	spring	autumn, spring	summer
Clematis (s, ps)	n/a	autumn	spring, summer or autumn
Colchicum autumnale (s)	n/a	summer	autumn
Convallaria majalis (ps, fs)	n/a	divide, autumn	late spring
Convolvulus cneorum (s)	spring	autumn	spring to summer
Cornus alba (s, ps)	n/a	autumn	year-round
Cotinus coggygria (s, ps)	n/a	autumn	year-round
Cotoneaster (s, ps)	n/a	autumn	year-round
Crambe cordifolia (s, ps)	spring, autumn	spring, autumn	spring, summer
Crocosmia cultivars (s, ps)	n/a	spring	summer
Cynara cardunculus (s)	spring	autumn, spring	summer, early autumn
Daphne (s, ps)	n/a	autumn, spring	late spring
Darmera peltata (s, ps)	spring, autumn	autumn, spring	autumn
Dianthus (pinks) (s)	n/a	autumn, spring	summer
Dicentra spectabilis ñ, ^ (ps)	spring	autumn, spring	late spring, early summer
Digitalis purpurea (ps)	late spring	autumn	early summer
Doronicum (ps)	spring	autumn	spring
Eccremocarpus scaber (s)	early spring	autumn	late spring to autumn

Camellia

Crocosmia

Plants	Sow	Plant Out	Season of Interest
Echinacea purpurea (s)	spring	autumn	summer, early autumn
Echinops ritro (s, ps)	mid-spring	autumn	summer
Elaeagnus (s, ps)	n/a	autumn, spring	year-round
Epimedium (ps)	n/a	autumn	spring
Eranthis hyemalis (s)	spring	autumn	winter, early spring
Erica cultivars * (s)	n/a	autumn	winter
Eryngium (s)	n/a	spring, autumn	summer, autumn
Eschscholzia californica (s)	spring, in situ	n/a	summer
Euonymus fortunei (s)	n/a	autumn	year-round
Euphorbia (s)	spring	autumn	year-round
Fatsia japonica (s, ps)	n/a	autumn, spring	year-round, autumn
Festuca glauca (s)	autumn, winter	spring, autumn	year-round
Filipendula (s, ps)	autumn, spring	spring, autumn	early summer
Forsythia (s)	n/a	autumn	spring
Fremontodendron ñ, ^ (s)	n/a	autumn, spring	spring to autumn
Fritillaria imperialis (s)	n/a	autumn	early summer
Fuchsia magellanica (s, ps)	n/a	autumn, spring	summer
Galanthus nivalis (ps)	n/a	autumn	winter
Garrya (s)	n/a	autumn	winter
Gaultheria procumbens *, ñ (ps)	n/a	autumn, spring	year-round
Geranium (s, ps)	spring	spring, autumn	early summer
Gunnera (s, ps)	spring, autumn	autumn	spring to autumn
Gypsophila ^ (s)	spring, in situ	autumn	summer
Hamamelis (s, ps)	n/a	autumn	winter
Hedera (s, ps, fs)	n/a	autumn	year-round
Helenium (s)	spring	autumn	summer
Helianthemum ñ, ^ (s)	spring	autumn	late spring, summer
Helichrysum ñ, ^ (s)	spring	autumn	late summer, autumn
Helleborus ñ, ^ (ps, s)	n/a	autumn	winter, spring
Hemerocallis (s)	autumn, spring	autumn	summer
Hippophäe rhamnoides ñ, ^ (s)	n/a	divide in spring	spring to autumn

Euonymus fortunei

Hedera

Plants	Sow	Plant Out	Season of Interest
Hosta (fs, ps)	n/a	autumn	spring to autumn
Houttuynia (s)	n/a	autumn, spring	spring
Humulus lupulus (s, ps)	summer	autumn, spring	spring to autumn
Hydrangea (s, ps)	n/a	autumn, spring	summer, early autumn
Hypericum (s, ps)	n/a	autumn, spring	summer
Ilex (s)	n/a	autumn, spring	year-round
Impatiens (ps)	spring	early summer	summer to autumn
Iris ñ (s)	n/a	late summer	spring, summer
Iris foetidissima (s)	n/a	late summer	early summer
Jasminum nudiflorum (s, ps)	n/a	autumn, spring	winter
Kerria japonica (s, ps)	n/a	autumn	spring
Kniphofia hybrids (s, ps)	n/a	spring, autumn	summer, early autumn
Lavandula (s)	spring	autumn	summer
Lavatera (s)	n/a	spring	summer
Leycesteria formosa (s, ps)	n/a	autumn, spring	summer to early autumn
Ligularia (s, midday shade)	autumn, spring	spring, autumn	summer
Ligustrum (s, ps)	n/a	autumn, spring	year-round
Lilium lancifolium *, ñ (s, ps)	n/a	autumn	late summer, early autumn
Liriope muscari (fs)	n/a	summer	autumn, winter
Lonicera (s, ps)	n/a	autumn, spring	summer
Lupinus slightly * (s, ps)	spring, autumn	autumn, spring	summer
Lysichiton (s, ps)	n/a	autumn	spring
Lysimachia (s, ps)	spring	autumn	summer
Magnolia (s, ps)	n/a	autumn	spring
Mahonia (fs)	n/a	autumn	winter, spring
Matthiola ñ, slightly ^ (s)	spring, summer	spring	late spring, summer
Meconopsis betonicifolia ñ, slightly * (ps)	spring, autumn	spring	summer
Mimulus (s, ps)	autumn, spring	spring	summer
Nepeta x *faassenii* (s, ps)	autumn	spring	summer
Olearia x *haastii* (s)	autumn, spring	spring	summer
Origanum ^ (s)	autumn, spring	autumn, spring	summer

Hydrangea

Lonicera

Plants for Your Garden

Plants	Sow	Plant Out	Season of Interest
Osmanthus burkwoodii (s, ps)	n/a	spring	summer
Osteospermum (s)	spring	spring	summer
Paeonia (s, ps)	n/a	autumn, spring	late spring to autumn
Papaver (s)	spring, in situ	autumn, spring	early summer
Pelargonium (s)	late winter	spring	summer
Penstemon cultivars (s, ps)	spring	autumn, spring	summer
Philadelphus (s, ps)	n/a	autumn	summer
Phlox annuals (s)	early spring	early summer	early summer
Phormium (s)	n/a	spring, autumn	year-round
Pieris * (s, ps)	n/a	autumn, spring	year-round
Primula bullyeana (ps)	spring	autumn, spring	summer
Primula denticulata (ps)	spring	early summer	mid-spring, summer
Primula vulgaris (ps)	spring	spring, autumn	spring
Pulmonaria (fs, ps)	n/a	autumn, spring	spring
Pyracantha (s, ps)	n/a	autumn, spring	year-round, autumn
Ranunculus ficaria (ps, fs)	n/a	autumn	early spring
Rheum (s, ps)	autumn	autumn	spring to autumn
Rhododendron * (ps)	n/a	autumn	spring
Rodgersia (s, ps)	spring	auumn, spring	spring to autumn
Rosa (s)	n/a	autumn	summer
Rosmarinus officinalis (s)	spring	spring, autumn	year-round
Rudbeckia (s)	spring	autumn	summer, autumn
Salix (s)	n/a	autumn	year-round
Salvia officinalis (s)	spring	autumn, spring	year-round
Santolina (s)	autumn, spring	spring, autumn	year-round, summer
Sarcococca (fs, ps)	n/a	autumn, spring	year-round
Saxifraga (s, ps)	autumn	spring	year-round
Scabiosa ñ, slightly ^ (s)	spring	autumn	summer
Sedum (s)	autumn	spring	early autumn
Sempervivum (s)	spring	spring	year-round

Primula

Pyracantha

Plants	Sow	Plant Out	Season of Interest
Skimmia (ps, fs)	n/a	autumn, spring	year-round
Spiraea (s)	n/a	autumn, spring	summer
Symphytum (s, ps)	autumn, spring	autumn, spring	spring
Syringa ñ, ^ (s)	n/a	autumn, spring	spring
Tagetes (s)	spring	summer	summer
Tamarix tetrandra (s)	n/a	autumn, spring	year-round
Taxus baccata (s, ps, fs)	n/a	autumn, spring	year-round
Thuja occidentalis (s)	n/a	autumn, spring	year-round
Thymus ñ, ^ (s)	spring	autumn, spring	year-round
Trillium grandiflorum *, ñ (s)	n/a	autumn, spring	spring
Trollius (s, ps)	spring	autumn, spring	spring
Tropaeolum speciosum ñ, ^ (s, ps)	n/a	autumn, spring	summer to autumn
Typha latifolia (s)	n/a	spring	summer
Verbascum ^ (s)	n/a	autumn, spring	summer
Viburnum (s, ps)	n/a	autumn, spring	winter
Vinca (s, ps)	n/a	autumn, spring	year-round
Viola odorata (s, ps)	spring	autumn, spring	late winter, early spring
Vitis coignetiae ñ, ^ (s, ps)	n/a	autumn, spring	spring to autumn
Weigela florida (s, ps)	n/a	autumn, spring	late spring, early summer
Yucca gloriosa (s)	n/a	spring	year-round
Zantedeschia aethiopica (s)	n/a	spring	late spring to summer

Trillium

Vinca

KEY

Plants marked with * require acid soil;

Plants marked with ^ prefer alkaline soil;

Plants marked with ñ prefer neutral soil.

(s) = sun

(ps) = partial shade

(fs) = full shade

Common Names of Plants

arum lily
  Zantedeschia aethiopica
baby's breath
  Gypsophila paniculata
bleeding heart *Dicentra spectabilis*
blue fescue *Festuca glauca*
broom *Cytisus and Genista*
bulrush *Typha latifolia*
busy Lizzie *Impatiens*
cardoon
  Cynara cardunculus
carnation *Dianthus*
catmint *Nepeta x faasseni*
cornflower
  Centaurea cinerea
cotton lavender *Santolina chamaecyparissus*
cowslip *Primula veris*
cranesbill *Geranium*
daylily *Hemerocallis*
dogwood *Cornus*
elephant ears *Bergenia*
firethorn *Pyracantha*
flag *Iris germanica*
foxglove *Digitalis purpurea*
hollyhock *Alcea rosea*
giant thistle *Onopordum*
globeflower *Ranunculus ficaria*
globe thistle *Echinops ritro*
guelder rose *Viburnum opulus*
hawthorn *Crataegus*
heartsease *Viola tricolor*
heath *Erica*
heather *Calluna vulgaris*
hellebore *Helleborus*
Himalayan blue poppy
  Meconopsis betonicifolia
holly *Ilex aquifolium*
ivy *Hedera*
lavender *Lavandula*
lesser celandine
  Ranunculus ficaria
lilac *Syringa*
lilyturf *Liriope muscari*
leopard's bane *Doronicum*
lupin *Lupinus*
mallow *Lavatera*
maple *Acer*
marigold *Calendula*
marsh marigold
  Caltha palustris

meadowsweet *Filipendula*
mock orange *Philadelphus*
mullein *Verbascum*
ornamental rhubarb *Rheum*
pink *Dianthus*
peony *Paeonia*
periwinkle *Vinca major, V. minor*
poppy *Papaver*
privet *Ligustrum*
purple loosestrife
  Lythrum salicaria
red-hot poker *Kniphofia*
red valerian *Centranthus ruber*
rock rose *Cistus, Helianthemum*
rosemary *Rosmarinus officinalis*
sage *Salvia officinalis*
scabious *Scabiosa*
sea buckthorn
  Hippophäe rhamnoides

Above: Ceanothus *thrives in a hot sunny position.*

snowdrop *Galanthus nivalis*
spindle *Euonymus*
spotted laurel
  Aucuba japonica
spurge *Euphorbia*
sweet box *Sarcococca*
tamarisk *Tamarix*
viper's bugloss
  Echium vulgare
wake robin *Trillium grandiflorum*
winter green *Gaultheria procumbens*
winter aconite
  Eranthis hyemalis
witch hazel *Hamamelis*
wood anemone
  Anemone nemorosa
yarrow *Achillea filipendulina)*

Index

Above: Dianthus *prefer alkaline soil.*

Index

Above: *Roses will tolerate a clay soil.*